Rick Mahorn

bullets

44

THE STORY OF THE WASHINGTON WIZARDS

Kyle Kuzma

A HISTORY OF HOOPS

THE STORY OF THE

WASHINGTON WIZARDS

JIM WHITING

John Wall

CREATIVE EDUCATION / CREATIVE PAPERBACKS

Published by Creative Education and Creative Paperbacks
P.O. Box 227, Mankato, Minnesota 56002
Creative Education and Creative Paperbacks are imprints of
The Creative Company
www.thecreativecompany.us

Design and production by Blue Design (www.bluedes.com)
Art direction by Rita Marshall

Photographs by Alamy (Cal Sport Media, ZUMA Press, Inc.), Corbis (Vernon
Biever, Clifford Ginsburg, Charles Tasnadi), Getty (Afro Newspaper/Gado,
Bill Baptist, Nathaniel S. Butler, Kevin C. Cox, Ned Dishman, G. Fiume, Focus
On Sport, John Iacono, Walter Iooss Jr., Mitchell Layton, Ronald Martinez,
Fernando Medina, Manny Millan, NBA Photo Library, Doug Pensinger,
Dick Raphael, Scott Taetsch, Jerry Wachter, The Washington Post), ©
Steve Lipofsky, Newscom (Ting Shen/Xinhua/Photoshot, Harry E. Walker),
USPresswire (David Butler II)

Library of Congress Cataloging-in-Publication Data
Names: Whiting, Jim, 1943- author.
Title: The story of the Washington Wizards / by Jim Whiting.
Description: Mankato, Minnesota : Creative Education and Creative
  Paperbacks, 2023. | Series: Creative Sports: A History of Hoops |
  Includes index. | Audience: Ages 8-12 |
  Audience: Grades 4-6 | Summary: "Middle grade basketball fans are
  introduced to the extraordinary history of NBA's Washington Wizards with
  a photo-laden narrative of their greatest successes and losses"--
  Provided by publisher.
Identifiers: LCCN 2022016897 (print) | LCCN 2022016898 (ebook) | ISBN
  9781640266469 (library binding) | ISBN 9781682772027 (paperback) | ISBN
  9781640007871 (pdf)
Subjects: LCSH: Washington Wizards (Basketball team)--History--Juvenile
  literature. | Washington Bullets (Basketball team)--History--Juvenile
  literature.
Classification: LCC GV885.52.W37 W55 2023 (print) | LCC GV885.52.W37
  (ebook) | DDC 796.323/6409753--dc23/eng/20220523
LC record available at https://lccn.loc.gov/2022016897
LC ebook record available at https://lccn.loc.gov/2022016898

Leroy Ellis

CONTENTS

LEGENDS OF THE HARDWOOD

As the 1978 National Basketball Association (NBA) playoffs began, hardly anyone paid attention to the Washington Bullets (who would become the Wizards nearly 20 years later). They had won just 44 games. Now they caught fire. They beat the Atlanta Hawks. Then they defeated the San Antonio Spurs and Philadelphia 76ers. Those teams had finished well above them in the Eastern Conference. They faced the Seattle SuperSonics for the NBA title.

Seattle won three of the first five games in the best-of-seven series. The average margin of victory in those games was just four points. Washington then blew out the Sonics in Game 6, 117–82.

The teams flew back to Seattle for Game 7. Washington took a 13-point lead into the start of the fourth quarter. Seattle whittled it to four with a minute and a half left. Bullets forward Mitch Kupchak scooped up a loose ball under the basket and put it in. He was fouled on the play. His free throw extended the lead to 101–94. Seattle narrowed the margin to 101–99. Just 18 seconds remained.

Seattle deliberately fouled burly Bullets center Wes Unseld. He was shooting just 55 percent from the free throw line in the playoffs. He calmly sank both shots. After a missed Seattle shot, Bullets forward Bob Dandridge raced downcourt to close out the scoring with an emphatic dunk. The final score was 105–99.

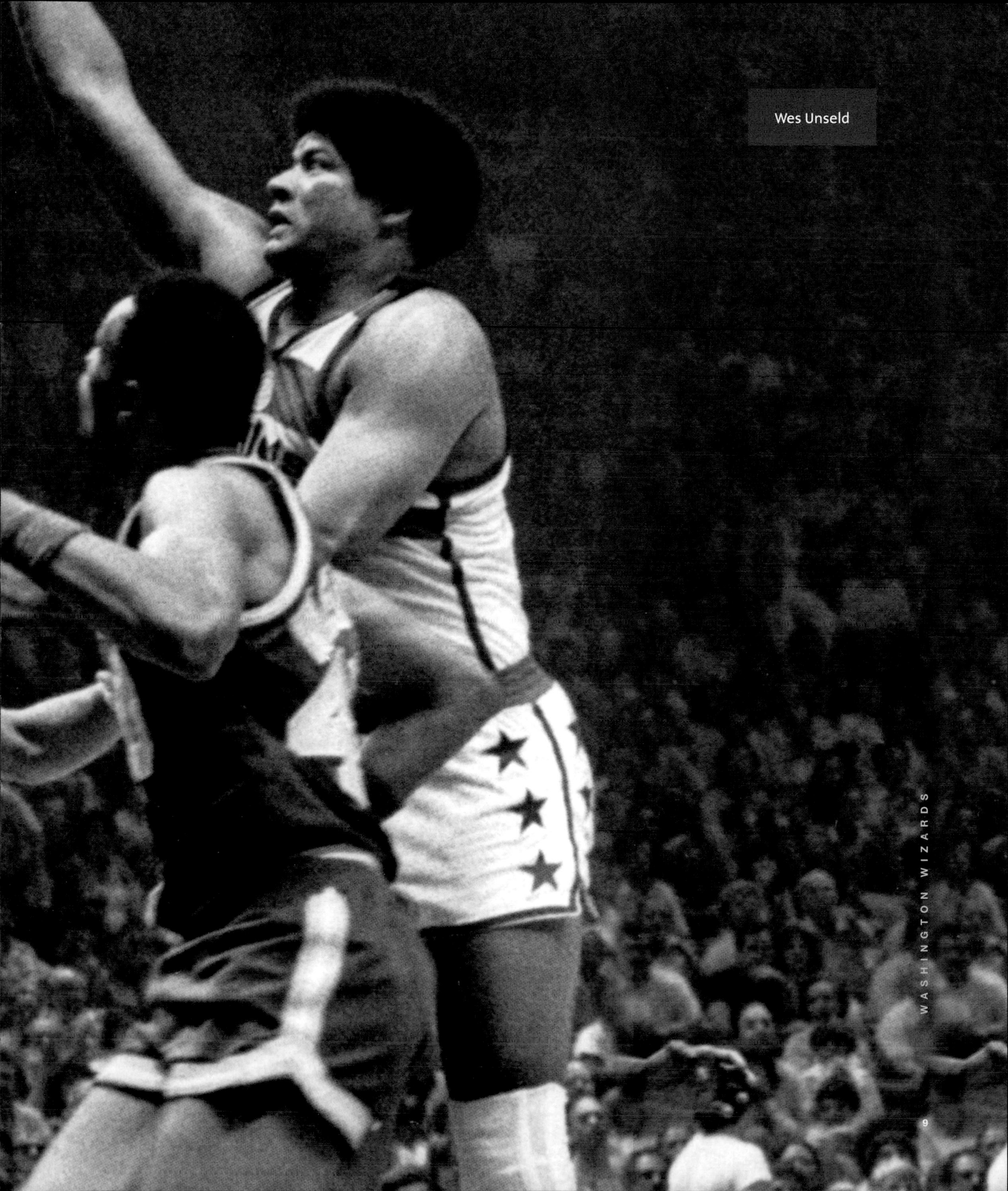

Wes Unseld

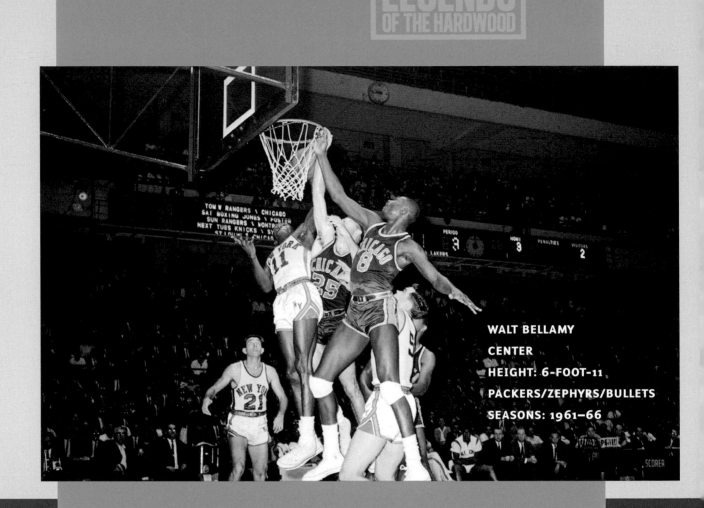

WALT BELLAMY
CENTER
HEIGHT: 6-FOOT-11
PACKERS/ZEPHYRS/BULLETS
SEASONS: 1961–66

OVERCOMING A RUDE RECEPTION

The Packers made Walt Bellamy the first overall choice in the 1961 NBA Draft. Early in the season, they faced the Philadelphia Warriors and dominating center Wilt Chamberlain. Bellamy introduced himself to Chamberlain. "You won't get a shot off in the first half," he replied. He rejected all nine of Bellamy's field goal attempts. As the second half began, Chamberlain said, "O.K., Walter, now you can play." The rest of the season went much better. "Bells" averaged more than 31 points and 19 rebounds a game. His 973 field goals are still a rookie record. He was NBA Rookie of the Year. He was also selected for the All-Star Game. He repeated that honor in the next three seasons.

The Bullets were NBA champions! They were just the third team to win a Finals Game 7 on the road. It would be 38 years before another team pulled that off.

That title-winning team was a far cry from the one that took the court for the first time in 1961 as the NBA's first expansion franchise. It was called the Chicago Packers, named for the city's meat-packing industry. The team didn't pack away many wins. Their 18–62 record was the league's worst. Center Walt Bellamy was NBA Rookie of the Year. There wasn't much talent around him. Six of Chicago's 10 top players were out of the league after the season.

Before the next season, the team changed its name to Zephyrs, after the Greek god of wind. Chicago is nicknamed the "Windy City." One reason for that nickname is the strong breezes that blow off Lake Michigan. The Zephyrs finished with only 25 wins. That poor record didn't draw many fans. The team moved to Baltimore, Maryland the following season.

The city was no stranger to pro hoops. A Baltimore team named Bullets was formed in 1944 in the American Basketball League and later became part of the NBA. The team won two league titles, but fell on hard times and folded early in the 1954–55 season.

When the Zephyrs arrived in Baltimore, they took on the Bullets name. The Bullets fired a lot of blanks the first season. They won only 31 games and didn't make the playoffs. But rugged center/forward Gus Johnson was runner-up for NBA Rookie of the Year. His future teammate Earl Monroe later commented, "Gus was ahead of his time, flying through the air for slam dunks, breaking backboards, and throwing full-court passes behind his back. He was spectacular, but he also did the nitty-gritty jobs, defense and rebounding."

Earl Monroe

BECOMING WINNERS

altimore had a losing record again in 1964–65. They made the playoffs, but lost to the heavily favored Los Angeles Lakers in the Western Division finals. Two years later, the Bullets won just 20 games. That gave them a high draft pick. They used it to take Monroe. He was a sensational point guard nicknamed "The Pearl." He was a real jewel who averaged more than 24 points a game. He was NBA Rookie of the Year.

The following season the Bullets drafted Wes Unseld. He was both NBA Rookie of the Year *and* Most Valuable Player (MVP) in the same season. Wilt Chamberlain is the only other player to achieve that feat. Though Unseld stood just 6-foot-7, he was immovable on defense and a dominant rebounder. "When we got Wes, we really got much better," Monroe said. "I think that gave us the impetus to know that we could win in this league." Win they did. The Bullets soared to a 57–25 record in Unseld's first season. But the New York Knicks swept them in the first round of the playoffs.

Baltimore lost to New York again in the 1970 playoffs. They got past the Knicks the following season in the conference finals. Now they faced the Milwaukee Bucks for the NBA title. The Bucks swept them. The Knicks knocked the Bullets out of the playoffs the following two seasons. By then they had added power forward Elvin Hayes. "The Big E" and Unseld gave the Bullets a dominating frontcourt. But the team still wasn't drawing fans.

The Bullets moved to Landover, Maryland before the 1973–74 season. Landover is only a few miles from the nation's capital of Washington, D.C. The team became the Capital Bullets. Once again, they lost to the Knicks in the playoffs. The Bullets had yet another name change before the next season. Now they were the *Washington* Bullets. "Located as close as we are to Washington, [D.C.] we think the name Washington is more definitive and provides a clearer identity to our actual location," said owner Abe Pollin.

The Bullets surged to a 60–22 record in 1974–75. After two hard-fought playoff series, they advanced to the NBA Finals. Washington was a heavy favorite against the Golden State Warriors. Yet the Warriors swept all four games. Two were decided by a single point. The Warriors won the other two by six and eight points. "It was very hard to take, considering how hard we had worked to get to the Finals," Hayes said. "But there was nobody in our locker room who wouldn't have wanted another shot at them. Let's face it: we thought we were better than they were."

Coach K. C. Jones

GUS JOHNSON
POWER/SMALL
FORWARD
HEIGHT: 6-FOOT-6
BULLETS SEASONS:
1963–72

Gus Johnson's college coach nicknamed him "Honeycomb" because his game was so sweet. Not everyone shared that opinion. "Gus was probably one of the roughest players I have ever played against," said New York Knick Dave DeBusschere. Johnson shattered three backboards with his explosive dunks. One came in 1964 when the Bullets played in St. Louis. The Hawks' owner sent Bullets' owner Abe Pollin the bill for repairs. "I tore it up," Pollin said. Johnson was a five-time All-Star. But he played before widespread media exposure. He was virtually forgotten. Former players kept insisting he belonged in the Hall of Fame. Their persistence paid off. He was enshrined in 2010.

WASHINGTON WIZARDS

LEGENDS
OF THE HARDWOOD

WES UNSELD
CENTER
HEIGHT: 6-FOOT-7
BULLETS SEASONS: 1968–81

HAVING AN IMPACT

Few players have had the same impact on their respective teams as Wes Unseld.
He used every ounce of his 245 pounds to compete with taller players for
rebounds and keep opposing players from driving to the hoop. Before his arrival,
the Bullets never had a winning season. During his 13-year career, the team
had 10 winning seasons and its lone NBA title. Five times the team won at least
50 games. Two of the losing seasons were his final ones, when knee problems
slowed him down. Since then, the team has had just 12 winning seasons. The
highest win total is 49. "I never played pretty," he said. "I wasn't flashy. My
contributions were in the things most people don't notice." Enough people did
notice to vote him into the Hall of Fame in the first year he was eligible.

TAKING THE TITLE THEN TAILING OFF

The Bullets had early playoff exits in the next two seasons. Fans had low expectations going into the 1977–78 playoffs. "The thing that happened with us that year is that we had a lot of injuries and one time we took a trip on the west coast and I had to use [assistant coach] Bernie Bickerstaff in practice," said coach Dick Motta. "I don't think we were overconfident, but we knew that we had a good team that would take a really good team to knock us out of the championship." Motta increased the intensity as the playoffs began. It paid off. "This is why we hung together and worked so hard," said a joyous Hayes after defeating Seattle. "That's why you play the game, and it was even better than you thought it would be."

The Bullets hoped for a repeat in 1978–79. They notched the league's best record. After series wins over the Hawks and the Spurs, they again faced the Sonics in the Finals. They won the first game, 99–97. Seattle swept the next four games.

Washington's glory days were over. They had two consecutive losing seasons. Unseld retired. Between the 1981–82 and 1987–88 seasons, they had winning records just three times. The most notable players during this time were center/ power forwards Jeff Ruland and Rick Mahorn. They were nicknamed the "Bruise Brothers" because they played so hard.

Surprisingly, the Bullets still made the playoffs in six of those seasons, though they were eliminated in the first round all but once. Their best performance came in 1988. The Bullets pushed the eventual conference-champion Detroit Pistons to a full five games in the first round. A one-point loss in Game 2 probably cost them the series. That series loss launched a long dry spell. The Bullets had losing records and missed the playoffs eight years in a row. They finally returned to the playoffs in 1997. The Chicago Bulls swept them in the first round.

WELCOMING THE WIZARDS

By the early 1990s, owner Abe Pollin became alarmed by the association of his team's name with gun violence. Washington, D.C. had one of the highest murder rates in the country. He became especially upset in November 1995. A gunman assassinated Israel's prime minister, Yitzhak Rabin. Rabin had been a close friend of Pollin's. Pollin announced a "rename the team" contest. Entries included Monuments, Antelopes, Funkadelics, Sea Dogs, and Stallions. "Wizards" emerged victorious.

The players liked it. "We're going to be the first Wizards team," said forward Chris Webber. "It gives us something that we have to make Washington proud of."

The name change became official before the 1997–98 season. The Wizards went 42–40 but missed the playoffs. They did even worse the following two seasons, finishing low in the league standings.

Chris Webber

MANUTE BOL
CENTER
HEIGHT: 7-FOOT-7
BULLETS SEASONS: 1985–88

TYRONE "MUGGSY" BOGUES
POINT GUARD
HEIGHT: 5-FOOT-3
BULLETS SEASONS: 1987–88

THE ODD COUPLE

In the 1987–88 season, the Wizards had one of the NBA's most unusual teammate pairings. One player was 7-foot-7 Manute Bol. He was one of the two tallest players in NBA history. Bol was a shot-blocking sensation. He wasn't much of a scorer. He is the only NBA player with more blocked shots (2,086) than points (1,599). The other was point guard Tyrone "Muggsy" Bogues. Standing just 5-foot-3, he was the shortest-ever NBA player. Despite his stature, Bogues blocked 39 shots in his career. He was much better-known for running the Bullets' offense. The two players had just one season together, in 1987–88. They were traded when it ended.

In 2000, Washington made headlines by hiring Michael Jordan as team president. He had retired two years earlier from the Bulls. The team also made another kind of headline. Its 19–63 mark was the worst since the first season in Chicago. Jordan laced up his shoes again for the 2001–02 season. "The way we'll be able to turn this around is to go out every night and have the effort," he explained. He helped the Wizards nearly double their win total to 37. They also won 37 games the following season.

ut despite Jordan's efforts, Washington still wasn't a playoff contender. He retired again. Without him, the team sagged to 25 wins in 2003–04.

The following season marked the start of a new era in Washington. The Wizards had traded for swingman Larry Hughes in 2002 and guard Gilbert Arenas in 2003. Now they acquired forward Antawn Jamison. They guided the Wizards to 45 wins. That was a 20-game improvement. They roped the Bulls in the first round of the playoffs, 4 games to 2. It was their first playoff series win since 1982. But the Miami Heat melted the Wizards in the next round. They swept all four games. The Wizards made the playoffs in each of the next three seasons. But the Cleveland Cavaliers eliminated the Wizards in the first round each time.

PUTTING UP A WALL

Arenas averaged well over 20 points a game for several seasons. But he missed most of the 2008–09 season with a knee injury. The Wizards limped to a 19–63 record. They weren't much better the following season. That record gave them the top pick in the 2010 NBA Draft. They took All-American guard John Wall. The losing continued though. Wall was injured at the start of the 2012–13 season. The Wizards lost their first 12 games without him. They finished 29–53.

The Wizards finally broke the losing cycle with a 44–38 mark in 2013–14. Wall was healthy for the entire season. He was named to the All-Star Game for the first of five consecutive seasons. The Wizards easily defeated Chicago in the first round of the playoffs. But the Indiana Pacers knocked them out in the next round.

Many people saw the Wizards as a team on the rise. "Washington is really becoming good right before our eyes," said Celtics president Danny Ainge before the 2014–15 season. "They improved a lot last year, and I think they're going to be a team that's going to be very good." The Wizards finished 46–36. They swept the Toronto Raptors in the first round. In the second round, they took a 2 games to 1 lead over the top-seeded Hawks. But they suffered three heartbreaking defeats in a row. They lost those games by five points, one point, and three points. Despite that setback, fans expected this recent run of success to continue in 2015–16. It didn't. Their 41–41 record missed the playoffs by three games.

John Wall

THE LAST HURRAH

Michael Jordan had a simple reason for returning to the hardwood: "I feel there is no better way of teaching young players than to be on the court with them as a fellow player, not just in practice, but in actual NBA games." For many of his new teammates, he succeeded. "He keeps the focus on us," said power forward Popeye Jones. "He came back to help this team, not to prove anything." He did prove that his skills were still there. At the age of 38 he became the oldest player to score at least 50 points a game. Age and creaky knees caught up with him. His two-year average of 21.2 points was far behind his 31.5 with the Chicago Bulls. Yet he led the Wizards in total points both seasons. As *Sporting News* writer Jordan Greer observed, "If anything, the final stretch of his career should serve as yet another reminder of just how great he was."

MICHAEL JORDAN

SMALL FORWARD

HEIGHT: 6-FOOT-6

WIZARDS SEASONS: 2001–03

Bradley Beal

Washington got back on track in 2016–17. They won 49 games as shooting guard Bradley Beal began the first of six consecutive seasons in which he averaged at least 22 points per game. They advanced to the conference semifinals. Boston defeated them, 4 games to 3. The Wizards made the playoffs again the following season. They fell in the first round to Toronto.

Washington dropped to 32–50 in the following season. They went 25–47 in the COVID-19-shortened 2019–20 season. Power forward Rui Hachimura was named to the NBA All-Rookie Second Team. They traded for point guard Russell Westbrook. He had three consecutive seasons of averaging a triple-double every game with the Oklahoma City Thunder, notching double digits in points, rebounds, and assists. Westbrook ended 2020–21 with his fourth

JOHN WALL
POINT GUARD
HEIGHT: 6-FOOT-4
WIZARDS SEASONS: 2010–20

A TROUBLED CHILDHOOD

John Wall's dad was in prison. Wall visited him almost every week. He died of cancer when Wall was nine. Wall was upset and furious. He often fought his classmates. "I had so much anger," he said. His bad attitude continued in high school. He disrespected his coaches. He had to repeat his sophomore year. He was even arrested. He did community service instead of jail time. Finally, he realized he needed to change. He focused on basketball. Colleges quickly noticed him. He chose the University of Kentucky and played one season. Then he entered the NBA Draft. The Wizards made him the first overall selection in 2010. Wall was named to the NBA All-Rookie First Team.

WASHINGTON WIZARDS

Kristaps Porziņģis

triple-double season. He also broke former superstar Oscar Robertson's career triple-double record. Westbrook's accomplishments seemed to spark the team. After starting 17–32, Washington went 17–6 the rest of the season to clinch a playoff spot. But they fell to the top-seeded 76ers, 4 games to 1, in the first round.

A familiar name to Wizards fans—Wes Unseld Jr.—joined the team as head coach in 2021–22. He guided the team to a 13–7 start. Center/power forward Kristaps Porziņģis came over in a trade not long afterward. He averaged 22 points and nearly 9 rebounds a game. In his first year with the team, shooting guard Kentavious Caldwell-Pope averaged more than 13 points a game. But Beal had wrist surgery and missed the second half of the season. The Wizards finished 35–47 and missed the playoffs. One loss was especially embarrassing. Washington led the Clippers 66–36 at halftime on January 25. Somehow the Clippers' Luke Kennard scored 7 points in the final 9 seconds. Los Angeles pulled out a 116–115 victory. To help the team return to the playoffs, with the 10th pick in the 2022 NBA Draft, Washington selected Wisconsin guard/forward Johnny Davis. The Big Ten Conference's Player of the Year averaged nearly 20 points per game as a sophomore in 2021–22.

Washington fans have endured some of the most dismal stretches in NBA history. Between 2008–09 and 2012–13, the Wizards won less than 30 percent of their games. Since then, fans' hopes have started to rise. They think that adding an outstanding rookie or a prized free agent would give them an excellent chance of a deep playoff run. They would love to see another championship banner hanging in Capital One Arena.

Kentavious Caldwell-Pope

INDEX